RELEASING THE ENTREPRENEUR IN YOU

A New Frontier for Christian Women

GERMAINE DUBLIN

Copyright © 2018 Germaine Dublin.

All rights reserved. No part of this book may be used or reproduced by any means, graphic, electronic, or mechanical, including photocopying, recording, taping or by any information storage retrieval system without the written permission of the author except in the case of brief quotations embodied in critical articles and reviews.

This book is a work of non-fiction. Unless otherwise noted, the author and the publisher make no explicit guarantees as to the accuracy of the information contained in this book and in some cases, names of people and places have been altered to protect their privacy.

Scripture taken from the New King James Version®. Copyright © 1982 by Thomas Nelson. Used by permission. All rights reserved.

Author available for speaking engagement.
Contact email germaine@jewelzondemand.com

CONTENTS

Synopsis vii
Dedication ix
Acknowledgements... xi
Introduction.. xiii

Chapter 1   Conquering Your Fear 1
Chapter 2   I Am an Entrepreneur....................................... 7
Chapter 3   Embracing Your Call 13
Chapter 4   How to Stay Motivated 19
Chapter 5   Ideas & Goals 27
Chapter 6   Minimum Viable Product and a Viable Business.... 33
Chapter 7   Business Plan 43
Chapter 8   Finances... 53
Chapter 9   Starting Your Business 61
Chapter 10   Branding.. 69
Chapter 11   Building a Website 75
Chapter 12   Email and Social Media Marketing and Analytics ... 83
Chapter 13   Managing Your Time...................................... 97
Chapter 14   Walking by Faith 103

Epilogue... 107

SYNOPSIS

She is seen as a strong woman. One that holds the family together. She is resourceful, and has the answers to almost everything. She is mother, wife, daughter, friend, hard worker and Sunday School teacher. You name it, and that's her. But she struggles with taking that next step to become an entrepreneur. She struggles with the very idea that this journey would mean time to work on her and what God has called her to do. She doubts her ability to walk a path mostly unknown to Christian women, and even more so, Christian women of color. She worries about not being viewed as "spiritual" by her family and church community because she is an entrepreneur and business woman. She draws back when she thinks of the opposition that she will face.

That woman has a name. She has purpose that is all her own. No one can live that purpose for her. She is determined to fulfill her calling in the marketplace. She recognizes that she has been called to walk a path that only she can walk. But she needs help in making those first few crucial and exponential steps.

Releasing the Entrepreneur in You: A New Frontier for Christian Women is written for that woman. Speaking in her very down-to-earth language, author Germaine Dublin will share the wisdom and expertise she has garnered as a Christian woman entrepreneur—and a woman of color. There are lots of good books on the market about entrepreneurship, but the Christian entrepreneurial women, especially women of color, have been an untapped potential. This book is specifically catering to these two groups of women. Christian women of color and Christian women in general are being challenged to be examples to those coming behind. They must step up to the plate to pave the way for the next generation of entrepreneurs.

Dublin will encourage, motivate and educate these women who have that desire to be what God has called them to be. She will debunk the myths that they have learned about women in relation to money, church and entrepreneurship and she will speak to the fears and anxieties of this woman. Finally, Dublin will outline the practical tools needed for that woman to start and run her own business successfully.

DEDICATION

This book is dedicated to my mother, Sarah Herbert Dublin, who has supported me and believed in me throughout all my life's endeavors. I love you dearly, Mum. Thank you for all that you have taught me, and for ensuring that I grew up to know that there is a God. You are an awesome mother and my wish for you is good health and long life.

I am also dedicating this book to the loving memory of an amazing woman, Liora Beer, whose recent passing has left such a void. From the moment I met you, I knew that you were different and had a heart for disenfranchised and marginalized people in our communities. I would have loved to present you with a copy of this book. I know you would have been so happy for me. Thank you for believing in me Liora. I do miss you.

ACKNOWLEDGEMENTS

To my two wonderful blessings, my children Shannon and Lenardo. You have been my inspiration. I love you without reservation.

To Thurlonne, Royston and Anique, you are so special to me. I cannot imagine life without you. I love you without end.

To my siblings, especially my brothers, Rudolph and Gregorie, thanks for looking out for me. You are awesome.

To my new son-in-law, Kadmiel Fenton II, welcome to the family.

Thank you to my spiritual teachers and pastors, Ishmael and Ruthlyn Bradshaw, who have imparted into my life for many years in such a profound way. You have also stood with me and prayed me through troubling times. Thank you for always being accessible in times of need.

To my current pastor and friend, Edris Webbe along with her husband Wilmoth Webbe, who has been my rock through some very difficult times. Thank you for encouraging me in my journey as an entrepreneur.

To Reuel and Christine Francis, I cannot remember a time when you were not there. Thank you for caring and for your support through the years.

To my cousins Hewlette, Jackie, Doannelda and Denlectro, and my forever friends Glanville White, Shaumen Gray, Carl Greenaway, Learie Cabey, Sharon Greenaway and all my other friends who have been there for me in one form or another. Thank you.

Thank you to Elder Marion Skeete who held my hands through the writing of this book. Thank you for seeing and believing in the vision.

To Ebenezer House of Worship family, I love journeying with you.

RELEASING THE ENTREPRENEUR IN YOU: A NEW FRONTIER FOR CHRISTIAN WOMEN

INTRODUCTION

Just think back to that time someone told you that you had a gift. Maybe it was someone from your childhood days—your school teacher, perhaps, or a family member. You seemed to be able to do this *thing*, whatever this *thing* is, so effortlessly. Then you grew up and a pastor, evangelist or prophet told you that God has called you to do this *thing*. The prophetic words resonated with you. Confirmation! Hallelujah!

The only problem is that no one clarified for you how this *thing* is going to be done. Furthermore, you have had no female entrepreneurs around you that you could emulate. You know it's within you, but you just don't know what to do with it. You even begin to wonder if this *thing* was not just a childhood fantasy. After all, entrepreneurship doesn't seem very "spiritual," or like "real ministry."

What has made it worse is that you might have told your husband about it or mentioned it to your pastor or church brethren, but no one seemed to take you seriously. No one listened or encouraged you—at least not the way you wanted them to. Or maybe someone did sort of take you seriously, but you began to doubt yourself about your call to entrepreneurship. You now look at your resume, your credentials and think someone must have been mistaken. This *thing* is too big for you. You don't have what it takes to do this *thing*. After a while, you begin to sound like Moses when God called him to lead the children of Israel out of Egypt. You say, "God I can't speak well. I have a speech impediment. I don't know how to do this *thing*. I am not a leader."

One thing you should know for sure is that God has a plan for your life. When he calls you, he qualifies you for the job. He has been preparing you all along, even in those seemingly unproductive seasons. Everything that you have done throughout your life has brought you to this place. Every experience has added to this moment and there are people out there waiting for you to come along and touch their lives. God has gone to great lengths to birth and nurture this *thing* in you. Your purpose is important!

I grew up in a Christian church. In fact, those who have known me might jokingly say, "You were born in church"—that's how much I attended! My grandfather was a deacon for many years and I went to church every Sunday and several times a week. I witnessed firsthand how unequally women were being treated in the church. In general, their ministry calling was not taken seriously. Over time there has been a shift in the church as a whole where women are now walking in their God-given gifts and talents. Some have even become pastors and leaders. But even though we have seen huge progress, many women have still not fully come to grips with the idea that they have been called to a specific purpose in the church, much less outside of the church in terms of entrepreneurship. "Marketplace ministry" is a concept that the church at large is still grappling with. However, it's really important for you to know that the *thing* that you been called to isn't any less spiritual because it is outside the church walls.

My hope for Christian women after reading this book is that they will feel empowered to follow their hearts, live up to their God-given calling, and launch the business they have been called to. I am a Christian woman who has ventured out to become an entrepreneur. Through trial and some failure, I battled my way through with the help of the Almighty God, family and friends. It took faith, perseverance and some guts, but it was worth it.

There are lots of good books on the market about entrepreneurship, but I believe that the Christian entrepreneurial women, especially women of color, have been an untapped potential. This book is specifically catering to these two groups of women. Christian women of color and Christian women in general are being challenged to be examples to those coming behind. They must step up to the plate to pave the way for the next generation of entrepreneurs.

Throughout this book I will speak to you from a place of transparency, and from a very unique perspective as a Christian woman of color within the church, as together we walk through the steps of becoming an entrepreneur.

The first section of this book will be a discussion about the spiritual strongholds and bondages that hold the Christian woman in places of slavery to unhealthy ideas about business and entrepreneurship, which consequently places her in perpetual need. The discussion will include scriptural references because it is important to know God's perspective on women in the marketplace.

The second section of this book will be looking at the logistics of starting a business. It will give you the tools needed to prepare and launch your business.

In the end you will be reminded that this walk is a faith walk. Once you have done your due diligence, it is the favor of God that will add the increase to the work of your hands.

I challenge you, if you are that woman who wants to live up to your full potential, be a successful entrepreneur, be an example to those coming after you, and leave a legacy for your children and grandchildren, this book is for you. There is a new frontier for Christian women. This is indeed a new day. It is time for you to finally start doing this *thing* you were called to.

SECTION 1

CHAPTER 1
CONQUERING YOUR FEAR

For God has not given us the spirit of fear, but of power and of love and of a sound mind. (2 Timothy 1:7)

Admittedly, I am one of those Christian women of color who for years battled with the idea of becoming an entrepreneur. As my outside-the-box ideas took root, I still struggled with the thought that I would be seen in the church as being fleshly, worldly, or carnal if I were to pursue entrepreneurship. I worried that at worst, I would be shunned, and that at best, I would not be encouraged or supported in my purpose. I wrestled with the idea that I would be seen as someone whose only interest was on making money rather than serving God, and that I was outside of the will of God in my pursuits. Because of living so many years with this erroneous belief, I felt like I would be sinning if I were to pursue this unique calling. I believe this came from the misinterpretation and misrepresentation of the scripture "For the love of money is the root of all kinds of evil" (1 Timothy 6:10). When I was growing up, this scripture was constantly misquoted as "Money is the root of all evil." This is clearly not what the scripture states, but I'm convinced that it has led so many women into believing that money is evil. Consequently, they are afraid to step out into entrepreneurship. You may be one of these women.

FEAR IS A HUMAN EMOTION

I was also gripped by fear as I contemplated entrepreneurship. Fear of the unknown. Fear of failure. Fear of being laughed at. Fear of wasting money. Fear of not knowing enough. Fear of not being good enough. I later found out that fear is not such an uncommon emotion. Fear is a normal human emotion, and we all have had the feeling of fear at some point in our lives. It is not a sin to feel fear and anxiety. Jesus did when he was in the Garden of Gethsemane. When it was coming close to the time for him to be crucified, he said to his Father, "Oh My Father, if it is possible, let this cup pass from me, nevertheless not as I will but as You will" (Matthew 26:39). It was quite evident that Jesus was feeling anxiety and fear, but he still went on to do the will of the Father. Jesus did not have fear of the unknown. In fact, he anticipated what was coming, but he knew what the flesh had to endure and would have preferred a different means of carrying out his purpose. Nonetheless, he was committed to doing what he was called to do. So, too, even when you and I feel fear, we must continue to do the will of the Father. The spirit of fear should not cripple us. Joyce Meyers is the first person who I heard say on one of her broadcasts that you may be afraid, but "do it afraid." She meant that you can acknowledge the fear, but do not let the fear control what you do.

BIBLICALLY BASED APPROACH TO FEAR

Perhaps you don't feel like you have the financial capital to start a business. Or maybe it's that you would be the first person in your family to even own a business. Whatever has generated the fearful situation in your life, here is my simple but biblically based approach for dealing with fear:

1. Tell God that you are fearful and why you are fearful. Ask him to help you get over the fear of stepping out in faith to become what he has called you to be. Ask him to help you put aside those unhealthy beliefs that you have about entrepreneurship, and replace them with healthy ones.

2. Rebuke the enemy by repeating applicable scriptures. Here are some scriptures you can use: "For God has not given us the spirit of fear, but of power and of love and of a sound mind" (2 Timothy 1:7). "Whenever I am afraid I will trust in you [God]. In God (I will praise His word), In God I have put my trust. I will not fear" (Psalm 56:3–4).

3. Start encouraging yourself in the Lord your God as David did (1 Samuel 30:6). Here are some encouraging scriptures that you can personalize: "And the Lord will make you the head and not the tail; you shall be above only, and not beneath, if you heed the commandments of the Lord your God" (Deuteronomy 28:13).

"For we are His workmanship, created in Christ Jesus for good works, which God prepared beforehand, that we should walk in them" (Ephesians 2:10). "I will both lie down in peace and sleep; for You alone, O Lord, make me dwell in safety" (Psalms 4:8). You have to let the enemy know that you know what the Word of God says. Jesus used the scriptures to rebuke Satan when he was trying to tempt Jesus based on his human vulnerability to fear.

4. The next step is to launch out with the fear. Do not wait for the fear to go away to do what God has asked you to do. The enemy, the devil, is the master of fear. If you wait for it to go away you will never start doing that thing you were called to do. You will find that as you walk in obedience to your calling, the fear dissipates.

5. Last but not least, believe that God is able to complete what he started in you. The words of Paul go like this: "Being confident of this very thing, that He who began a good work in you will complete it until the day of Jesus Christ" (Philippians 1:6).

God expects obedience from us. When God calls you to do a thing, he expects you to do it. Some may not believe this is an obedience issue, but it is. The scripture has been quite clear in 1 Samuel 15:22 that "to obey is better than sacrifice." Obedience is not an option. It is a requirement.

Your obedience is also for the benefit of those who are waiting to be touched by your purpose. It is for those young women and little girls coming behind who need a role model, someone to emulate, and someone to hold their hand and show them the way. Look around in your churches and see how many women entrepreneurs are in your midst; how many can you call a role model? Probably not many. At the end of the day, obedience will conquer fear. So be obedient and push beyond your fear.

CHAPTER 2

I AM AN ENTREPRENEUR

Before I formed you in the womb I knew you, before you were born I sanctified you; I ordained you as a prophet to the nations. (Jeremiah 1:5)

Having gained a better understanding of how to master your fear, you are now able to think more clearly about what God has called you to do. Believe that God has a plan for your life. Upon reflection, you may realize that the experiences you have had throughout your life, the people that you've met, and the opportunities that you've been given, have all brought you to this day. You may have questioned God and yourself because you did not understand why you were having some of these experiences. It is now beginning to make sense to you. It's all coming together. God has been preparing you for entrepreneurship.

It was God who brought different people into your life to teach you some things that you needed to know. He wanted to strengthen you, so he allowed you to live through the experiences that you did. God has had a hand in this all along. Isn't it wonderful to know this? If you are still uncertain about your calling to do that thing—to be an entrepreneur—see the checklist below. This can help you decide or firm up your resolve.

- Are you a risk-taker? Are you always looking for something different or new to put your energies into?
- Do you like being in control? Do you like being your own boss?
- Do you feel like you are different than others and do not quite fit in?
- Are you a good leader and a good listener?
- Are you organized and disciplined with money?
- Do you think outside of the box and seek ways to take action on ideas?
- Do you like making money?
- Do you feel most content and happy when you are doing what you like, even if it requires more time and effort?

- Do you feel like God has called you to something?
- Have you had words spoken into your life that lines up with your other experiences?
- Do you feel like even though you try to do other things, you always end up back at the same place or juncture and faced with the decision to do that "one thing"?

If you answered yes to most or all of the above questions, then entrepreneurship is very likely for you. Recognizing that entrepreneurship is for you is the first step—and a very important step—in your entrepreneurial journey. Make no mistake: entrepreneurship is not a walk in the park, and there are many pitfalls along the way. You can avoid some of these pitfalls if you are aware of the challenges that can lead to these pitfalls and choose to mitigate them. Below is a list of some of the challenges to entrepreneurship that I have experienced in my journey—some or all of which you will experience in yours:

- You will work harder and longer hours than when you were in your regular job—if you are not careful, that is.
- You will make costly mistakes. Be very wise about your spending and decision-making. Seek advice when expedient.
- The business will drain your finances. You may have to eat out less and reduce your household expenses.
- Family and quality alone time will be affected. Make time for family and yourself.
- You may not be able to take a lengthy holiday for a long time. Try to do less costly vacations, i.e., go to another state instead of going overseas.
- You may not get the support from family and friends like you thought you would. So don't expect too much.

- People may not like your product or care to pay for your service, which is why you get people's input early on, so that you can streamline your offerings. That said, your product is not for everyone.
- You are not able to build your business the way you would like initially. Limited resources is key here, so manage them well.
- Running the business requires a lot of discipline. Have good habits. Spend 80 percent of your time on things that bring in money and 20 percent on other administrative things. Delegate administrative work if you can, or outsource them if you can afford to.
- You will second guess yourself, wondering if you made the right decision. This happens to everyone, so don't be thrown off by it. Remind yourself you are on a God-given assignment.

The list above is not exhaustive, but it can help you to prepare mentally for the journey. In addition, here are some realistic statistics that you need to know as part of your preparation:

According to the U.S. Small Business Administration, over 50 percent of small businesses fail in the first year of business and 95 percent fail within the first five years. While this may be true, if you have the right motivation and determination, you would not let this scare you. You will be in the successful 5 percent, once you allow God to lead you.

BENEFITS OF BEING AN ENTREPRENEUR:

1. You will be your own boss.
2. You will be building your own business and not someone else's.

3. Your earnings may increase with hard work and making the right choices. This will allow you to be better able to take care of your family.
4. You will have more flexibility with time management. This is important, especially if you have small children.
5. You will feel a great sense of achievement when you build a successful business.
6. You will constantly be learning new things and be challenged to grow.
7. You may be able to provide employment for others.
8. Last but not least, you will experience the joy and contentment of walking in the favor and will of God.

All of the above are really great benefits to being an entrepreneur. However, the final questions I would like to ask you is, What does your gut say to you? What is it that you *know*, that you *know*, that you *know* that God has called you to? Listen to that inner voice that tells you things that you sometimes do not want to acknowledge for one reason or the other. That voice that you have tried to ignore is more than likely the voice of the Holy Spirit. However, while all these are legitimate concerns, I will say if you really want to have a different experience in life and do that *thing* that God has called you to, like Steve Harvey says, *You've got to jump*. There is just no other way. You've got to act on faith and *jump*. Harvey continues by saying that when you jump, your parachute may not open right away, and you may hit the ground, but know that God is with you. You simply must make that jump—that leap of faith.

CHAPTER 3

EMBRACING YOUR CALL

The heart of her husband safely trusts her, she willingly works with her hands, she also rises while it is yet night, She considers a field and buys it, plants a vineyard, she extends her hands to the poor; Her children rise up and call her blessed. (Proverbs 31)

I would like you to think of your calling to become an entrepreneur as a divine calling. It is not simply you pursuing your dreams; it is you answering a call. It is a calling by God to a higher purpose. As such it should be embraced, even coveted. A successful entrepreneurial woman is an asset to the church, her community, her family and to her God. She invests wisely. She builds, lives and leaves behind a legacy for her children. Her children call her blessed and her husband trusts her. Because of her entrepreneurial spirit, she will be a financial blessing to those in need. She shows discipline and is an example, a teacher and a mentor to others.

It is not so much what you want to do; there is a divine will that is involved here. It is what *God* wants you to do. There is a path that you are called to walk. We all know the popular scripture, "For I know the thoughts that I think toward you, says the Lord, thoughts of peace and not evil, to give you a future and a hope" (Jeremiah 29:11). God was speaking to the Children of Isreal specifically, but he was also making a point beyond that time and context. He knows everything about *you*. He made plans for you long before you are even able to carry out those plans. It is for you to recognize that you are on assignment for God and be obedient to this call.

Please know that women are called to many things, be it in the church or outside of the church. You may have been called to start a business, or you may have been called to be a Sunday School teacher, or both. As I mentioned before, ministry is not only to be done within the walls of the church. Ministry is also being in the marketplace, positioning yourself so that you are able to help the church carry out its evangelistic and discipleship mission by spreading the good news, as well as by your financial investment. These are vitally important roles, just as it is to hold an office in the church. You should be in a position to lend and not to borrow. Furthermore, no longer should the church have to be always looking to the world for charitable contributions to support our godly agenda. The world is not interested in our godly agenda. God has given everyone gifts to use for his purpose, and that is to reach the lost, poor and dying. That is not the world's agenda. However, the wealth of the world can be used for kingdom building.

I really want to debunk the myth once and for all that the only way or only place we can do ministry is in the church. I would like to draw your attention to a story in the book of Acts where the twelve disciples eventually came to the decision to have seven men oversee the distribution of food to the needy widows because they were not able to continue doing this chore themselves. They chose to continue preaching and discipling others, while others tended to the widows. The twelve disciples instructed the other disciples on the qualifications these seven men needed to have to be considered for this position, and they were the same criteria for pastors, evangelists, teachers of the word, and deacons. The criteria was that they needed to be filled with the Spirit, full of faith, and be of good character. After the seven men were chosen, *hands were laid upon them* and they were blessed for service. Clearly, distributing food to the widows was not seen as any less important than preaching and discipling. Hands were laid upon them because they were being anointed and commissioned for ministry! Although the characters in this example were men and not women, the message is the same for you. While entrepreneurship may not be seen as a "spiritual vocation," under God, the criteria for carrying out this service is no different from any other position that you may hold in the church. Once you are in the will of God, whatever you do is spiritual.

Before you embark on doing anything, first seek God to find out what his assignment or will is for your life. Your assignment is going to look different to another person's assignment. Just allow God to lead you and you will come to fully realize and walk in your purpose. This may mean that you are going to have to let go of some of the ideals and presumptions you may have had. You will have to put to death some of the crippling and misleading "truths" you may have learned in your earlier years about Christian women becoming entrepreneurs.

YOU, TOO, CAN BE BI-VOCATIONAL!

Contrary to what may have been popular belief, the Bible actually documents female entrepreneurs who simultaneously held positions in the church. So, they were, in a sense, bi-vocational. In Acts 18:3, it is documented that Priscilla was a tentmaker along with her husband, while being a missionary and helping with the early Christian Church. Acts 16:14 speaks of Lydia being a dealer in fabric and also a worshiper of God. She is a great example that you can be an entrepreneur and at the same time give yourself wholeheartedly to worshiping God. Deborah was the fourth judge in Israel, while at the same time she was a prophetess and a politician (referred to as an agitator). She was very active in things outside the "church" that may not be seen as spiritual by some but they all concerned the advancement of the kingdom of God (Judges 4). I will urge you to look up these scriptures and read them for yourself and be encouraged by them. It doesn't have to be either-or. It can be both-and. God may choose to call you for service both within and outside the church. You, too, can be bi-vocational.

As with these women entrepreneurs in the Bible, God also has a plan for you. So the questions to you are, What has God called you to? How long have you been procrastinating? I will admonish you to not put it off any longer. You can do it in incremental steps:

1. Start by putting your thoughts down on paper.
2. Try to have a single focus. This can be tweaked when you get to building your business plan.
3. Narrow down your to-dos into actionable small steps.
4. Do your market research. Find out first if the service is really needed and who needs it. You will refine your niche market in your business plan.

5. Carve out time to work on these actionable steps.
6. See what you can get help with – who is on board with you.
7. Continue reading this book to the end as it contains valuable information on how to take your dream forward.

CHAPTER 4

HOW TO STAY MOTIVATED

Be strong and of good courage. Do not be afraid; nor be dismayed, for the Lord your God is with you wherever you go. (Joshua 1:9)

By now you might be getting even more excited about the idea of being an entrepreneur. That is a good thing. You need to cherish these feelings of excitement because you are going to have to revisit these feelings as time goes by. You will face challenges in business or even as you get into the throes of starting a business. As that glimmer of hope and promise begin to kindle in your soul, fan those flames with your eagerness to fulfill your calling. The time will come when you'll need to remind yourself of the day when you fully embraced your calling to do this *thing*. You'll need to remember when you started to believe that what was elusive all along is now possible. You are going to be an entrepreneur. You are going to fulfill your purpose. You finally feel whole. You are on the right track.

Entrepreneurship requires a huge amount of commitment because it will affect the way you live. It is going to dictate where and how you eat to the type of vacations you take. Everything about your life will be affected. You may have to curtail certain habits and learn to say no to a lot of things, including fun things and family outings. This may feel discouraging to you, especially as you will not have experienced success as yet.

There may be other things to discourage you along the way, such as lack of support from family or friends. It would be to your best interest to remember from the get-go that the vision is yours. Not anybody else's. The earlier you realize and accept this, the better you will be able to do what is needed to grow your business. You are going to find that family, friends and even church brethren are not going to support you the way you might have thought. You will not have the investment in the business from others that you would like. But that is okay. It truly is, because some support could prove to be problematic in the end, but that's a different story for another book!

I will urge you, however, not to expect others to act like your business is their business too. If you have a supportive partner or children, that's great, but do not get upset if they do not give up their lives to run your business with you. What I would suggest is that instead of seeking huge investment from your family or friends, have them be responsible for one task, instead of two or three. Or maybe they can help with occasional tasks as their time allows. Or maybe they just want to invest some cash but not be hands-on in the business. Every situation is different. If I were to use my situation as an example, my daughter keeps my accounts payable and receivables, and at the end of the year, gets everything together for the accountant. This is a huge help because I would not have had the time to do this as well. It is better to have her do this, than have her be overwhelmed from doing too much. The morale of this story is, do not put too much pressure on those around you because if you do, they will disappear. You would want to have some support around you to keep you motivated, so don't alienate your family and friends by having unrealistic expectations.

MOTIVATIONAL TIPS

Listed below are some other tips that you may want to consider implementing that can keep you motivated:

- Celebrate small successes. Do not wait for the big ones or you may become discouraged.
- Be sure to start off with good habits to balance work and home life. You don't want to get burnt out.
- Get yourself an accountability partner. This is someone that you can trust who will hold you to your timelines and help you balance your life.
- Get a mentor if you can. This person may serve as your accountability partner, too. But if not, it is okay if you have a variety of people. You can use each of them to get ideas. They can help you avoid some costly mistakes and they can offer you some better ways to do things.
- Surround yourself with positive people. People who are going to encourage you. These are not "yes" people, but people

who can give constructive advice. Do not be constantly in the company of people who do not appear to be doing anything positive with their lives or people who criticize often. People who are never able to give compliments or give good advice. They will pull you down eventually.

- Make sure to do your homework. Keep abreast of what is happening in the relevant markets. Take note of what the competition is doing. This can give you an edge.

- Get a good amount of sleep at night because this would help you to feel refreshed the next day. You don't want to feel tired all the time. Tiredness can affect your mood and judgement.

- Do not neglect your diet and exercise. They keep you energized and avoid putting on weight. You will feel better about yourself if you do.

- Try to remember why you are doing this. You can put a quote above your desk or pictures of your family on your desk. This may help you to remain focused on the important things in life.

- Finally, remember to make time to pray daily. Ask God to help you and to guide you. Read the scriptures. Know some encouraging scriptures that you can repeat to strengthen your resolve to continue. Here are some scriptures to reflect on: "Fear not, for I am with you; Be not dismayed, for I am your God. I will strengthen you, yes, I will help you; I will uphold you with my righteous right hand" (**Isaiah 41:10**); "But those who wait on the LORD shall renew their strength; They shall mount up with wings like eagles; They shall run and not be weary, they shall walk and not faint" (**Isaiah 40:31**); "Trust in the LORD with all your heart and lean not on your own understanding; in all your ways acknowledge to Him, and He shall direct your paths" **(Proverbs 3: 5-6).**

Congratulations! You have completed the first section of this book. Hopefully you are ready to go forward into the second section of this book, where you will learn how to start your own business and also learn some steps to growing your business. If you are not ready and need to read the first section again, please do so. If you are ready to forge ahead, then let's do this *thing!*

SECTION 2

CHAPTER 5
IDEAS & GOALS

For which of you, intending to build a tower, does not sit down first and count the cost, whether he has enough to finish it. (Luke 14:28)

Releasing the Entrepreneur in You

I want to applaud you for getting this far in your entrepreneurship preparation. Now that you have settled your doubts, learned how to deal with your fears and anxieties, let's move on to the more practical things. One thing that has been mentioned earlier and is necessary to reiterate, is that becoming an entrepreneur requires commitment. It's not going to happen by prayer alone. Luke 14:28 says that if we want to build a tower, we must sit down and estimate the cost to see if we have enough money to complete it. In other words, we need to be practical and count the cost before any major undertaking. Entrepreneurship is not magic, nor is it an event. It is a journey and you are entering unchartered territory. There are actionable steps that you are going to have to follow through on. Solicit the support of your close family and friends if you can. You can be successful without them, but it could be that much easier having them on board, depending on the business you are getting into. As a child of God, you will need him to guide you every step of the way. You have to be committed for the long haul. Be determined to get up after a fall and continue on your journey.

You have entered into section two of this book where we are going to discuss the practical steps that you will need to take to start and run your business. You will be given information on business planning, finance, and marketing. You will be provided with information on free resources to help you get your business going. I will also give you snippets of my journey and highlight some of the mistakes that I made. This is to help you not to make these same mistakes and to encourage you to continue.

FORMULATING YOUR BUSINESS IDEAS

For some of you reading this book, this may be a time of upheaval in your life. You may have just gone through a divorce or separation and need to increase your income. Perhaps your children have left home or gone off to college. Maybe you are dissatisfied with your job because you believe that you are called to something better, bigger or greater. Or you may just want to supplement your income. Whatever the case, you now have to reinvent yourself and set new goals for your life and for the business that will become an integral part of your life. For some of you, the goals are not just for yourselves but for your children and family and the other young women who are looking up to you.

You are wondering where to start. You may have so many ideas swirling around in your head. Decide on the direction you want to pursue in your business and start formulating your ideas on paper. As you write your ideas down, you will be able to make sense of them. Don't worry about perfection or having it all correct in the first instance. As you go along, you will revisit and adjust these ideas.

PERSONAL GOALS FOR THE BUSINESS

Before you start to do anything, think about what your personal goals are for this business. Do you want your business to be full-time employment, a part-time job or a side hustle? Do want to be working from home because your commute to work is too long? Do you have small children and the babysitters are too expensive, or do you prefer to home school your children but want to bring in some revenue to help your husband with the bills at the same time? No one can tell you what you want from this business. You have to decide that for yourself because the risk is all yours. Once you have decided on what you want from this business, then you will be able to decide how much money you will need to make to live comfortably being self-employed, or how much you need to supplement your primary income, or how much you need to help your husband meet the demands of the household. In other words, *What are your financial goals for this business?*

BUSINESS GOALS

So what are these ideas that you have for a business? What is your business going to be? Businesses are centered around a problem. Think of it this way. There is a problem or a pain point, as it is sometimes called, that people are experiencing. Your business is going to solve that problem. That is your main goal. Although you want to make money, and lots of it, money is not your main goal. Your job is making life easier for others. This is the first goal that you are going to commit to paper, along with your ideas on how to correct the problem. State clearly what the problem is and how you are going to fix it in an efficient and cost-effective way that would appeal to potential customers.

FINANCIAL CAPITAL GOALS

Another challenge you may have is capital. Depending on the type of business, you may need quite a lot of money to start, or you may not. Service-oriented businesses tend to cost less. If you are offering a physical product, then it typically will cost more. Money is usually very scarce for entrepreneurs in the beginning. At this stage of your business, the banks and other institutions will not lend you any money. There are, however, other ways to get money, but you will have to do some financing out of pocket in the beginning. You are the first investor. No doubt, you would need to decide on the finances you need to start your business. This is another goal that you will have to decide on before you launch your business.

We will discuss financing further in a later chapter and look at ways to raise capital. The reason for mentioning financing in this chapter is because when you are thinking of starting a business, you have to think of your financial goals for the business. It's not just what you want out of it, but also what you have to put into it to get it up and running. When I started my first business, I did not have any concrete written goals. I found myself in the thick of things trying to figure out financial goals. I did not have any training at the time.

All I knew is that I wanted to do business. I wanted to be my own boss. Mistakes can be costly, both in finances and wasted time. So figure out your financial goals sooner rather than later before you make the same mistake.

BREAK EVEN GOAL

There are other goals that you will need to think of that will be discussed further along in your business plan—such as timelines. What are your projected timelines to achieve a particular outcome? For example, what are your projections for breaking even? That is to say, within what timeframe will you have made back all the money that was invested in your business so that you will truly begin to make a profit? This will help you determine how much business you need to do or products you need to sell, to make that amount of money to reach the goal within the timeframe you decided on.

STAY ON TRACK

Staying on track with your goals is not always easy. It requires discipline. Getting an accountability partner, or better yet, a mentor, preferably one who has a business, can be a plus. Some people have also contracted coaches to help them while they are building their business. Coaches can be costly, so that is something to think about. But if you can afford one, I would say, go for it. Research the coaches well before making a choice. Look at their online profile to see their reviews. See if people like them or get good value for the money paid. Look at how long they have been a coach or have been working in the related businesses. Word of mouth could be good if it is from someone you trust, or even from the masses. Whatever you do, put checks and balances in place to keep you on track.

CHAPTER 6

MINIMUM VIABLE PRODUCT AND A VIABLE BUSINESS

Who can find a virtuous wife? For her worth is far above rubies. (Proverbs 31:10-31)

You have identified what the problem is and how you are going to solve that problem. The next step is for you to work on your offerings, which is your product or service that is going to be used to solve the problem. If you plan to produce physical items for sale or provide a service, you will need to make sure that you can make a viable business out of that product or service. The business needs to make money. To ensure viability, make a sample of your product and test your idea out to see how people respond to your product. Do not produce too many items of your product up front, until you know if people like it and will pay for it. Also, do not offer too much variety. This makes it very difficult for you to manage, and in addition to that, when people are presented with too many choices, they get overwhelmed and will not buy. Limiting the variety of products will also allow you to be able to determine the best sellers.

If you are going to provide a service, I would advise that you to do a survey to find out if the service is something that people would need. You may want to ask friends and family, although sometimes they may not be the best people to ask. Friends and family may be biased, or they may not feel comfortable telling you the truth. Whether it is a product or service, strangers may be better to use, so that you can get impartial feedback. Pay attention to the way you word the questions. You want the participant to feel like the questions are not directed at them in a manipulative or intimidating way, so that they can offer feedback freely and generally. Here are some key questions to ask:

- Is this a product or service that you think people would want or need?
- If there was anything you could change about the product or service, what would it be?
- If you were to purchase this product or service, what would you consider to be a reasonable price to pay for it?

GETTING FEEDBACK

Asking questions like these is the hard part for some people. It can be difficult to listen to criticism, however constructive. Honestly, this is the best exercise you can do before you start investing heavily in the business. In fact, you don't want surveys to be a one-time activity. You would want to continue asking customers and random people their opinion periodically, even after you have started your business. This could help you immensely to improve your offerings, if you ask the correct questions and if you use the information wisely. What you don't want to happen going in to a business is for everyone to give you the thumbs up, and you go ahead and invest lots of money in a product that no one buys.

Many business owners believe that constructive feedback is the best thing that anyone can do for their business because it gives them an edge. It gives them the "meaty nuggets" they can use to improve their product, which hopefully translates into sales. You must have that mindset also. SurveyMonkey.com is a free app that can help you with conducting surveys. It is free to a point. You will be charged depending on how many times you use it in a month and how many participants are involved in the survey. The surveys on Survey Monkey are customizable, so you can tweak the questions to suite your purpose.

GETTING A PATENT

If you are producing technology that has not been used before, it is advisable to get a patent to protect the right to the idea. Be careful to keep certain information private before you start the process to patent your product because you don't want anyone to steal your idea and start making your product themselves, whilst you are in the development stage. Copycat behavior can easily happen when other businesses notice that your product has the potential to be profitable or is profitable. The big companies can undersell you and put you out of business or they can patent your product themselves if you have not done so. Patenting costs money and it takes time, but if you have done your research and you think it can make a viable business, then go for it.

As a sidebar, there are companies out there that will pay to have your idea patented if they believe your product will be profitable. One of the downsides is that you may not have ownership of the product. You may get royalties but always read the fine print and consult a lawyer to make sure that you are properly represented in a contract.

GETTING A COPYRIGHT

This is a way to protect the way your work is expressed and not specifically the idea. People can and will steal your work if you do not get a copyright. Seek legal advice for this. You may copyright your book, music, art, movies, photographs, advertisement, illustrations and patterns. You can file registration online at copyright.gov.

GETTING A TRADEMARK

This protects symbols, phrases, pictures and words that distinguish your products or business from other businesses. Things like your logo, tag lines and product names should be trademarked. This prevents other people from using your name or logo to sell their products. You can get independent legal advice by retaining an attorney or go to legalzoom.com for online legal advice. Legalzoom may be cheaper.

HOW TO DETERMINE BUSINESS VIABILITY

So how do you really determine if something is viable? As mentioned before, you would do surveys. However, you really may not know if your business is viable until you actually start selling your products. In some cases, though, technology and innovative products can attract buyers before production is complete. This would allow you the opportunity to have huge pre-sales that may meet your targets. There are also times when people are offered incentives to buy services before a business is launched. Again, this would be a good indicator if a business is viable or not. If these two scenarios mentioned above do not exist, then you would have to do your best to make projections based on what your needs are, and determine if the business can meet its financial goals.

To determine viability, you would have to first set your financial goals.

1. You want to have two monthly financial goals:

    a) How much money do you need per month from the business to keep it going? What is your minimum cash flow requirement?

    b) How much money would you like to make so that you can live the life that you want? What is your ideal revenue for the month?

2. Once you have answered the questions above, then you need to determine how you are going to price your product or service.

    a) Pricing your product is fairly easy. You add up the cost of the materials used, plus the cost of the time it took to make the product, plus all packaging and marketing costs (essentially you add all costs associated with producing the product) and multiply by 4, if you will be selling your product retail; or multiply by two, if you are selling wholesale. When you are working out the costs you do not add things like rent, electricity, cleaning etc. because these will be accounted for when you multiply the cost by two or by three. This formula applies if you are making the product yourself. If someone else is making it, then it would be easier because the cost of producing the product will be the price that you pay to get the product from someone else.

b) When you have done all your calculations, you need to determine how many pieces of your goods or items you need to sell weekly or daily to meet your minimum revenue requirement for the month. If you are selling different items and the costs vary, use the price of the most costly product to do your calculations.

c) If you are providing a service, look at the time you need to prepare and deliver the service to that client. This includes your prep time, travel time, telephone consulting time and follow-up. If you were to look at your minimum revenue requirement for the month and decide on the cost per hour to do all of the above, this will tell you how many clients you need to have per month to get you to the minimum monthly revenue goals. Once you have worked that out, you multiply this figure by two. Here again, you are not going to add rent and administrative services because they will be accounted for in your calculations.

3. After having done the above exercise, if you are falling short of getting your minimum monthly requirement, it is either that you are not charging enough for your services or you need to have more clients. However, the time allocated to doing work for your paying clients should not fall outside of the forty-hour week. That is not to say you will not work more than forty hours sometimes, but if you need to work more than forty hours to get to your minimum monthly requirement, then I would advise you to adjust your pricing. If you are still not hitting that mark of your minimum requirements, then the business is not viable.

A little word of advice: There are entrepreneurs who believe in charging clients for their time when they are providing a service. People are not interested in paying you for your time. They are interested in outcomes. When you are pitching your business or marketing, you need to show people the benefit of working with you. They need to see what your product or service can do for them—whether it will help them save money or in some way make their lives easier. Your product or service needs to solve a problem. This idea cannot be stressed enough. Your time means nothing to your clients if they do not get favorable outcomes, or if you are not solving their problem. Of course to be able to invoice someone, you may need to work out the costs by the hour, especially if you are working with them for a period of time, possibly months. However, let them know how much it will cost to accomplish their goal and then break it down into billable units.

MARKET RESEARCH

Market research is very important when determining business viability. When you are deciding on pricing your product or services, you will want to look around and see what other people in similar industries are charging for their products and services. If the other vendors in the marketplace are offering similar products at a much cheaper price, you would need to look at what you can do to make your price more marketable. People will not buy if the prices are too high. You must be able to justify your costs. It may mean that you have to look at where you are sourcing your materials and find cheaper vendors. If there are other reasons why the product or service is charged at a higher price, you need to be able to communicate this value to the client.

In some other cases, especially when charging for a service, pricing can become more tricky. Businesses often charge for their services, depending on the perceived value this service is going to bring to the client. So if they think that the service being offered is going to put the client in a place where they are going to earn a lot of money, they charge a higher price. If the business is not a potentially big moneymaker, they charge less.

Determining the value of your product or service can be difficult. I remember struggling for some time with pricing my products. There will be people who will want to sow seeds of doubt about your pricing and make you feel like you are charging too much. You have to know the worth of the product or service you provide. Don't let anyone dictate your pricing to you. Remember that pricing your product or services right is crucial to making your business a viable one.

CHAPTER 7
BUSINESS PLAN

There are many plans in a man's heart nevertheless the Lord's counsel - that will stand. (Proverbs 19:21)

Building a business plan is a very important step in starting and growing your business. A business plan is like a road map, a paradigm, if you will. You use it to assess the progress or failure of your business. If your business is not going according to plan, you will be able to assess the situation very early on to find out why the business is not meeting its goals. You may find that you need to make a slight shift in your game plan and change the way you do some things.

A good business plan takes time to put together. It can be as simple as you want it to be, or as detailed as you want it to be. Certainly, if you plan to approach a bank or lending institution, you would need to have a lot of detail, especially around the finances. Lenders and investors always want to know how they are going to recover the money that they lend to you, and then some!

There are quite a number of business plan templates available, and most experts agree on the essential components of a traditional plan. Bear in mind, however, that the key purpose of any business plan is to allow you to put processes in place to run your business effectively and to help you determine if you have a valid business concept. It is recommended that you have a twelve-month profit and loss projection, a cash flow projection, a projected balance sheet, and a break-even calculation.

In the initial stages of the business planning, I would suggest using the template from leanstack.com. This does not have as much detail as a traditional business plan, but what it does is tease out all the important issues. It covers nine areas—from products to how you plan to make money. Provided for you below is The Small Business Association outline of the essential parts of a traditional and lean model business plan. Choose which type of plan works best for you and use it. There's no right or wrong way to write a business plan. What's important is that your plan meets your needs.

Most business plans fall into one of two common categories: traditional or lean startup. Traditional business plans are more common, use a standard structure, and expect you to go into detail in each section. They tend to require more work upfront and can be dozens of pages long.

Lean startup business plans are less common but still use a standard structure. They focus on summarizing only the most important points of the key elements of your plan. They can take as little as one hour to make and are typically only one page.

TRADITIONAL BUSINESS PLAN

This type of plan is very detailed, takes more time to write, and is comprehensive. Lenders and investors commonly request this plan. The plan falls into two categories: a Lean Business Plan and a Lean Startup Plan. This type of plan is high-level focused, fast to write, and contains key elements only. Some lenders and investors may ask for more information.

TRADITIONAL BUSINESS PLAN FORMAT

You might prefer a traditional business plan format if you're very detail oriented, want a comprehensive plan, or plan to request financing from traditional sources.

When you write your business plan, you don't have to stick to the exact business plan outline. Instead, use the sections that make the most sense for your business and your needs. Traditional business plans use some combination of the following nine sections:

EXECUTIVE SUMMARY

Briefly tell your reader what your company is and why it will be successful. Include your mission statement, your product or service, and basic information about your company's leadership team, employees, and location. You should also include financial information and high-level growth plans, if you plan to ask for financing. This should be written last.

COMPANY DESCRIPTION

Use your company description to provide detailed information about your company. Go into detail about the problems your business solves. Be specific, and list the consumers, organizations, or businesses your company plans to serve.

Explain the competitive advantages that will make your business a success. Are there experts on your team? Have you found the perfect location for your store? Your company description is the place to boast about your strengths.

MARKET ANALYSIS

You'll need a good understanding of your industry outlook and target market. Competitive research will show you what other businesses are doing and what their strengths are. In your market research, look for trends and themes. What do successful competitors do? Why does it work? Can you do it better? Now's the time to answer these questions.

ORGANIZATION AND MANAGEMENT

Tell your reader how your company will be structured and who will run it.

Describe the legal structure of your business. State whether you are or intend to incorporate your business as a C or an S corporation, form a general or limited partnership, be a sole proprietor or LLC.

Use an organizational chart to lay out who's in charge of what in your company. Show how each person's unique experience will contribute to the success of your venture. Consider including resumes and CVs of key members of your team.

SERVICE OR PRODUCT LINE

Describe what you sell or what service you offer. Explain how it benefits your customers and what the product lifecycle looks like. Share your plans for intellectual property, like copyright or patent filings. If you're doing research and development for your service or product, explain it in detail.

MARKETING AND SALES

There's no single way to approach a marketing strategy. Your strategy should evolve and change to fit your unique needs.

Your goal in this section is to describe how you'll attract and retain customers. You'll also describe how a sale will actually happen. You'll refer to this section later when you make financial projections, so make sure to thoroughly describe your complete marketing and sales strategies.

FUNDING REQUEST

If you're asking for funding, this is where you'll outline your funding requirements. Your goal is to clearly explain how much funding you'll need over the next five years and what you'll use it for.

Specify whether you want debt or equity, the terms you'd like applied, and the length of time your request will cover. Give a detailed description of how you'll use your funds. Specify if you need funds to buy equipment or materials, pay salaries, or cover specific bills until revenue increases. Always include a description of your future strategic financial plans, like paying off debt or selling your business.

FINANCIAL PROJECTIONS

Supplement your funding request with financial projections. Your goal is to convince the reader that your business is stable and will be a financial success.

If your business is already established, include income statements, balance sheets, and cash flow statements for the last three to five years. If you have other collateral you could put against a loan, make sure to list it now.

Provide a prospective financial outlook for the next five years.

Include forecasted income statements, balance sheets, cash flow statements, and capital expenditure budgets. For the first year, be even more specific and use quarterly — or even monthly — projections. Make sure to clearly explain your projections, and match them to your funding requests.

This is a great place to use graphs and charts to tell the financial story of your business.

APPENDIX

Use your appendix to provide supporting documents or other materials where specially requested. Common items to include are credit histories, resumes, product pictures, letters of reference, licenses, permits, patents, legal documents, and other contracts.

EXAMPLE TRADITIONAL BUSINESS PLANS

Before you write your business plan, read these example business plans written by fictional business owners on the US Small Business Administration website. "Rebecca owns a consulting firm, and Andrew owns a toy company."

LEAN STARTUP FORMAT

You might prefer a lean startup format if you want to explain or start your business quickly, your business is relatively simple, or you plan to regularly change and refine your business plan.

Lean startup formats are charts that use only a handful of elements to describe your company's value proposition, infrastructure, customers, and finances. They're useful for visualizing tradeoffs and fundamental facts about your company.

There are many versions of lean startup templates, but one of the oldest and most well-known is the Business Model Canvas, developed by Alex Osterwalder. You can search the web to find free templates of the Business Model Canvas, or other versions, to build your business plan.

The following are the nine components of the Business Model Canvas version:

KEY PARTNERSHIPS

Note the other businesses or services you'll work with to run your business. Think about suppliers, manufacturers, subcontractors and similar strategic partners.

KEY ACTIVITIES

List the ways your business will gain a competitive advantage. Highlight things like selling directly to consumers, or using technology to tap into the sharing economy.

KEY RESOURCES

List any resource you'll leverage to create value for your customer. Your most important assets could include staff, capital, or intellectual property. Don't forget to leverage business resources that might be available to women, veterans, Native Americans, and HUBZone businesses.

VALUE PROPOSITION

Make a clear and compelling statement about the unique value your company brings to the market.

CUSTOMER RELATIONSHIPS

Describe how customers will interact with your business. Is it automated or personal? In person or online? Think through the customer experience from start to finish.

CUSTOMER SEGMENTS

Be specific when you name your target market. Your business won't be for everybody, so it's important to have a clear sense of who your business will serve.

CHANNELS

List the most important ways you'll talk to your customers. Most businesses use a mix of channels and optimize them over time.

COST STRUCTURE

Will your company focus on reducing costs or maximizing value? Define your strategy, then list the most significant costs you'll face pursuing it.

REVENUE STREAMS

Explain how your company will actually make money. Some examples are direct sales, memberships fees, and selling advertising space. If your company has multiple revenue streams, list them all.

For free business plan templates, you can go to the Small Business Association website, where you will find both traditional and lean model canvas templates.

Below are additional free business plan templates found in Resource Toolkit by Mario Farleo:

- **Bplans** – The largest online collection of free sample business plans. Also provides helpful tools and guides to help you better manage your business.
- **Bplans's Gallery of Samples** – Over 500 examples of business plans.

- **Oprah.com's One Page Template** – Get one-page business plans for a small consulting business, a boutique clothing company and a nonprofit organization.

- **Score's General Model Startup Template** – Business plan template for a startup business, with instructions for each section and fillable worksheet.

CHAPTER 8
FINANCES

Moreover it is required of stewards that they be found faithful. (1 Corinthians 4:2)

Before you embark on your business, you need to think of how you are going to finance it. When I started my business, I did not do my homework properly and even though I got someone to help me with a business plan, I paid no attention to the plan, and certainly not the financials. It was a big mistake because I just slipped further and further down into a financial abyss. I was dipping heavily into my personal finances and damaged my personal credit. I was putting the needs of the company before my personal needs, which meant that my own bills would not get paid on time. Some say that bad credit is a casualty of being an entrepreneur. Sure you can rebuild your credit, but try to avoid ruining your credit in the first place, if you can. If you run your business this way, you will get frustrated. Creditors will be calling you and you won't be able to afford to do some things that you want to do because of the financial constraints. The other downside is that you are going to have to rebuild your credit to get financial support from lenders in the future.

TIP:

Do not mix your business account with your personal account. Keep them separate. This is better for tax and reporting purposes.

HOW TO GET FINANCING FOR YOUR BUSINESS

- **Personal savings.** Be careful and use only what you are willing to risk losing. Another word of caution: do not mortgage your house or tap into your pension if you are not absolutely certain that your product or service is a sure thing. However, bear in mind that no lending institution or serious lender will lend you money if you have not invested your own money in your business.

- **Home equity line of credit.** This is easier to get. The interest rate is lower than an unsecured loan and interest may be tax-deductible.
- **Micro loans.** This an opportunity for family and friends to lend money in a non-threatening way. The idea is that you would have them each lend you small amounts, for example $500.00 - $5000.00, depending on your needs. You would offer them a percentage return on their lending (people tend to use 10 percent but it could be whatever you choose). Give them a time frame for return, such as one year. Draw up a simple contract if you want, nothing complicated. This would let your investors know that you are serious, and it will give them some peace of mind. Usually the person who is lending the money is really the responsible party to provide a contract. So you do not need to provide a contract; you will do so only if you want to.
- **Bank loans.** In the initial stages, banks will not lend you money for your business. You would need to be in business for at least three years for them to consider you for a loan.
- **SBA loans.** Small Business Loans (SBA loans) are small-business loans guaranteed by the SBA and issued by participating lenders, mostly banks. SBA loans are guaranteed by the government—meaning you get long terms with the lowest rates.
- **Crowd funding.** There are a number of sites online that offer crowd funding. These are just sites that ask people to lend small amounts to people like yourself. There is usually a target amount that you want to reach, which will be published on the site. The loans have to be repaid, but with no interest. If you are interested, do your research for the best crowd funding sites. You are expected to put together

Releasing the Entrepreneur in You

a campaign that normally runs for thirty days. A couple of popular sites to use are **Kiva.com; kickstarter.com.**

- **Angel investing.** These are individuals who invest capital in startup businesses that appear viable with a view to converting the debt or for ownership equity.

- **Venture capitalists.** Although this happens down the line when the business is profitable, venture capitalists look for a strong management team, a large potential market, and a unique product or service with a strong competitive advantage. These are companies trading in millions of dollars.

- **Mission-based lenders.** These are organizations that lend money from governments and non-profits. The loans are geared toward building up disadvantaged communities. They usually have a 501(c) (3) status. **Accion** is one such organization.

- **Early purchase.** This is where to get family and friends to purchase or pay in advance for your services or products prior to starting your business. You must show them the benefit of signing up early. You can offer an incentive, i.e., a special price for those who sign up with you in advance.

How you manage your day-to-day finances is very important in business, especially as a startup. Remember that the monies you receive have to be repaid, and in most cases, with interest, so you don't want to waste it. Keep close tabs on your spending. This cannot be stressed enough. Below are some tips on how to curtail your spending.

TIPS ON HOW TO MANAGE YOUR DAY-TO-DAY FINANCES

1. Stick as far as possible to your business plan until you have identified in your monthly or quarterly assessment that you need to shift your spending from one area to another.
2. Negotiate your terms with vendors early. Try and get the best deal. Do your research, however, to make sure you are getting the best bang for your buck. If you can consolidate, then do so. It may be cheaper to use one vendor to provide two to three services, instead of two to three vendors, providing the same things separately.
3. Try not to lock yourself into long-term binding contracts unless you think that it is too good to pass up. But I have a rule: if it sounds too good to be true, it probably is.
4. Try to keep costs down as much as possible. For example, if you're a service provider, why not use your home office or your home as an office to cut down on overheads? Do not get "brick and mortar" involved in the initial stages, if you do not need to. You can meet a client at Dunkin Donuts or Starbucks. There are also some spaces being made available in some cities where you can rent for a period of time to do whatever you want, such as meeting clients.
5. Stick to your budget when buying the resources you need, and do not overspend. I can speak for myself. I love stationary, especially uniquely beautiful stationary. Every time I go into the stationary store I want to pick up something. There was a time I would just buy stationary for the sake of doing so, but then I looked around and thought, *Just how many journals, sticky pads and pens do I need?* Just remember the costs all add up.
6. You don't need new furnishings. The old desk is fine, unless of course it's falling apart. Purchase secondhand furniture

in the beginning. There are always people who want to get rid of office furniture. Visit a secondhand store or even ask family and friends. Someone may have a desk or chair they want to get rid of to make space in their home or office, but do not want to throw it away because it is in good condition.

7. File your taxes on time so you don't get charged. In some states such as Massachusetts you are required to pay a state tax in addition to federal tax. The state tax is mandatory irrespective of whether or not you made a profit that year.

8. Pay attention to your bank account, so it does not go into overdraft and you get charged a fee. Pay your other bills on time, if possible, to avoid unnecessary charges.

Your business plan is the roadmap of your business and the finances is the heartbeat of your business. You need to ensure, or at least try to ensure, that you maintain a healthy balance sheet by paying attention to both.

CHAPTER 9
STARTING YOUR BUSINESS

Faith without works is dead. (James 2:17)

After all the preparation you have been through, you have finally come to the exciting part. You are about to register your business. Think of it as a new day!

TIPS TO STARTING AND RUNNING YOUR BUSINESS

1. **Register your business.** This is done through your local government website. As mentioned earlier in the business plan, you would need to know what type of business you are going to be—an LLC, S-Corp, C-Corp, partnership or sole proprietor. This is important because you would need to pay taxes and the type of business you have will help to determine how much taxes you pay.

   Also, clients need to know that you are legitimate, especially if you are pitching to a wider audience. You will also find that some vendors will only engage with you if you are registered and can present them with an EIN number. The EIN number will be allocated to you when you register your business and will serve as the identifier of the business.

   You would need a physical address when registering the business. This could be your home address, if you do not have a physical business address.

2. **Open a business bank account.** Have a bank account for the business that is separate from your personal account. Think of a business as a person. As a person, the business finances has to be handled separately. So even though you have the "right" to handle the finances and make decisions for the business, you have to do what is in the best interest of the business. If you use the business finances inappropriately, you will be held accountable.

   As you did when registering the business, you can use your home address to open the business bank account after you have registered the business. You cannot use P.O. boxes to register a business or open a bank account.

3. **Find a workspace and/or build a website.** Determine a space for doing your business, whether it's at home or a designated business place. Having a physical space or storefront is expensive and comes with its own responsibilities and liabilities. For example, the landlord will want to lock you into a contract for a few years. These contracts could be tenuous. Even if the business is not making money, you are tied into that lease. I would advise not to lease unless you have a product that absolutely needs to be in a store. Try other options such as a website or social media sites, or you can try to get your products into other stores or boutiques.

4. **Be found.** People need to know you exist. Start some social media accounts. You have so many choices these days. Facebook, Instagram, Twitter, Pinterest, Periscope and Linkedin are some of the more popular ones. There are lots of others. Use whichever site you think is beneficial to your business. Some sites work better, depending on the industry you are in. For example, if you are selling physical products, Linkedin and Twitter may not be the best choices. Facebook and Instagram would be better. However, if you are a public speaker and looking to be hired by a company, Linkedin is best.

Search engines such as Google, Bing and Yelp are places you want to register your business. This would make it easier for your business to be found. You do need a physical address to register on these sites. It is not advisable to use your home address for social media and search engine sites because the address will be displayed online and random people may show up at your home. There are virtual addresses you can use to register your business online. These virtual offices can offer you additional services, such as taking calls and

Releasing the Entrepreneur in You

collecting messages, collecting and forwarding mail, or both. You just need to do your research for whatever suits you. Use of a virtual address usually costs a small fee per month.

5. **Keeping books.** Start off with a good accounting system in place. You do not need a big accounting program initially, unless the amount of financial activity warrants one. You can use an Excel spreadsheet. When the business grows, and you think you need an upgraded accounting program, you can upgrade. In most cases, Excel can be transposed into these other programs, so you do not have to re-enter the data into a new program. I am saying this because you might be thinking it would save you time and money to get the fancy program earlier rather than later, because it would cost you more in the long run. No, it will not, because Excel is compatible with Quick Books and other accounting programs too. Check the program you want to use beforehand for compatibility.

After you have done that, you would need to identify someone who will do your accounting for you. Here again, do your research. A good accountant can save you lots of money. Have a consult with the accountant early and let them advise you on what to do. Usually accountants offer the first consultation for free. You need to interface with an accountant, as you do not want to file your taxes late because the business will be penalized. The IRS will charge you. Also, some states, such Massachusetts, charge you state taxes, which is a set fee per year. You will also be penalized in this state, if you don't file on time.

6. **Staffing.** Having the right people to help your business is critical. You want an effective staff or team.

    (1) For some business owners, in the beginning phase you may be the receptionist, bookkeeper, marketing lady,

cleaner and the one to carry out the service that the business offers, but that is okay. If you are not sure what your staffing needs are, give yourself some time to sort it out. You may not have much business when you begin, so you do not need anyone. However, as you grow and demands increase, you can look at hiring someone.

(2) Consider outsourcing some parts of your work. This can help keep costs down and reduce time. There are websites that offer services by freelance workers for little or manageable costs. Consider this—when you take on a staff member you will have to pay a salary, whether you make money or not. In addition, you have to pay benefits; you need to find space (although some work can be done remotely); and you possibly need additional equipment for them to work; and the list goes on. So don't employ staff until you absolutely need to.

(3) You can use interns to help you do some of the work. Some universities offer that option for their students that need to get work experience. You can go on a university website and see if they offer interns and take it from there. Usually the intern works for free and you just need to provide them with a letter of recommendation at the end. The interns are usually free of cost for up to three months. If you go beyond their internship period, then you may have to pay them, and you are then able to work out a renumeration package. One downside to this option is the lack of continuity. Interns are available for three months at a time, which usually means high staff turnover and you will be interviewing very often in order to have someone at all times. Also, you do not know the quality of work you will receive.

7. **Non-profit.** Similarly, for those who are doing non-profits, there is a different staffing structure that is required by

Releasing the Entrepreneur in You

law to keep you accountable. The monies that are used to fund these businesses are usually public funds. As a result, transparency is at the forefront of how you manage the business and the funds given to you. Non-profits are tax free and so the IRS wants to make sure that the business is accountable. Not much will be discussed about non-profit organizations in this book, but if you are interested in starting a non-profit, you may want to speak with someone who is familiar with the process of completing the 1023 form so that you can acquire the 501(c)(3) status, which is a charitable status. This process can take from two to twelve months to come to completion. Let me end by clearing up one misconception about non-profit businesses: You might have heard that you will not make any money running a non-profit. This is not necessarily the case. The financing structure will be different because you will need to be actively seeking out funding, mostly grants, to run this business, but you will get paid.

8. **Cash flow.** Make sure that you have enough cash to keep your business afloat and manage your spending as discussed in chapter 8.

9. **Marketing.** You would have already outlined your marketing plan in your business plan. Put your marketing plan into action. Remember, however, that this is just a plan. In the initial stages you may not know exactly what will work for you or your business, but you have to start somewhere. Keep a keen eye on your social media marketing so that you will be able to identify what works well and what does not. Pay keen attention to your analytics as well, because they can help you market more effectively. Marketing will be discussed further in an upcoming chapter.

CHAPTER 10
BRANDING

~~~

But you are a chosen generation, a royal priesthood, a holy nation, His own special people. (1 Peter 2:9)

In simple terms, branding just means that you are providing a means for clients to recognize you in the marketplace. People will get to know you and your business by getting to know your name and your logo. Think about Nike. Whenever or wherever you see that famous Swoosh, you know it is a Nike product. This is what you want to happen for your business. Very early on in your business, get a logo that you will associate with the name of the business (by this time you would have already named your business). This does not have to be expensive. There are lots of free sites to help you design your own logo. A list of resources have been provided at the end of this chapter for your convenience. The sites are either free or inexpensive. You want to make sure that you like the logo before you start using it because you will be stuck with it.

The logo is to be used on your business cards, letterheads, websites and across all social media sites. Use your logo in postings on your sites as well. Put your logo on bags, pens, T-shirts and any paraphernalia associated with the business.

When choosing a logo, things to take into consideration are the colors that you use, as different colors prompt different feelings about the business. For example, red speaks to boldness and youthfulness, so if you are targeting the youth, this may be a good color to use. Blue is dependability and strength; yellow is charitable and warm; green speaks of growth and health; orange speaks of cheerfulness and confidence. Look around you and take notice of the colors that other businesses use and see how they correspond to the message they have been portraying. This is important, when you know the clients you want to attract. In my research and observation, I discovered that baby pink does not generally appeal to professional women, nor does blue generally appeal to teenagers. This is why on my website jewelzondemand.com, that is targeting women, you would not find baby pink on the logo.

Branding is not just about the symbols that people see, but also about what it represents. When people see your blue logo, they need to be thinking that your business is dependable. You want good characteristics to be associated with your brand. Brands tend to focus on certain characteristics and highlight them, not only through the colors they use, but they highlight them in their marketing.

Pay attention to the grammar you use. Go to gramerly.com to get help with your grammar. Your graphics must be of good resolution. They must not be stretched or fuzzy. PowerPoint, Canva and Google Graphics can help with that. Be consistent with colors, fonts, wording and what you are talking about. Be consistent with spacing. These details may seem inconsequential, but they have impact on how well your message, product or service is received.

Branding is also about the kind of service you provide. It speaks to your responsiveness and your reliability. If you offer poor service, this is what people will think about when they see your logo. This is one of the reasons why you have to pay attention to your brand reviews online and try to resolve the issues quickly. People do look at reviews and use the information to determine if they should buy or not buy. If people consistently see bad reviews, they are going to associate them with your brand.

Key players that are associated with your brand need to also have good characteristics because it can harm your brand. Very recently the name Wynn was removed from the Wynn Casino in Boston. This is because the person whose name is in the brand was accused of bad behavior and the stakeholders wanted to distance themselves from the Wynn name. You are the face of your brand, so be careful what you do, because whatever you do will be associated with your business.

RESOURCES TO HELP DESIGN YOUR OWN LOGO

- 0 to 255 – Find variations of any color.
- Canva – Amazingly simple graphic design software that helps even non-designers create stunning layouts and graphics.

Releasing the Entrepreneur in You

- Chalkmark – Improve your user-experience and get quick feedback on designs with this free usability testing software.
- Color Picker – Chrome extension that lets you identify any color's hex code on any website.
- Craft – A free UI design plugin designed to speed up your workflow with Sketch and Photoshop.
- Designinspiration – Pinterest made exclusively for designers—a resource to help you discover, share and save your favorite designs from around the web.
- GIPHY – Find, share or create your own gifs.
- Mockup.io – Visualize and collaborate on mobile app design.
- InVision – Web and mobile prototyping tool and UI mockup tool. Perfect for collaborating on web designs and working through feedback.
- Logaster – Online logo maker and generator.
- Marvel – Mobile and web prototyping for designers.
- MockFlow – Online wireframe tool and design cloud for software and websites.
- MoodBoard – Build beautiful moodboards for sharing designs, inspiration and ideas.
- Niice – Private moodboards where you can gather, share and discuss ideas with your team.
- Placeit – Place your app or website directly into one of these free iPhone, iPad, iMac and Macbook mockups (no Photoshop required). They offer thousands of photo and video templates.

- Signature Maker – Create a handwritten digital signature. Great for signing documents, contracts, emails and blog posts.
- Squarespace Logo – Free logo building tool for Squarespace users.

CHAPTER 11
BUILDING A WEBSITE

Test all things; hold fast what is good. (1 Thessalonians 5:21)

Releasing the Entrepreneur in You

Websites can be costly, especially if you are building a custom website. There are, however, lots of platforms available now that can offer you great websites that are much easier to use and cost much less. Website builders such as wix.com and squarespace.com and other websites listed at the end of this chapter, offer a number of attractive templates for different types of industry/business that you are in. Think about the cost of building your website. Do your research. Ask around. You may know someone who knows someone that can build a very good website for you without charging you an arm and a leg.

A website needs a host and a domain name. A domain name is what the website is called. For example, my business domain name is jewelzondemand.com. First, check to see if the name you want is available for you to purchase. You can do so by going on to sites such as Host Gator, Blue Host, Go Daddy and Dream Host and type in the domain name that you want. If the domain name is available you would see a cost attached to it. The cost of the domain names can range from $1.99 to thousands of dollars. Only pay a higher amount if the domain name is that valuable to you. Otherwise, keep looking until you find a name that you can work with, and is affordable.

Hosting is a service that allows individuals and organizations to post their web pages or websites onto the internet. The host of your website keeps your information on a server so that when your domain name is typed into a browser, your website would pop up and potential customers can access your information. There is a cost for hosting which is usually paid on an annual or bi-annual basis. When you are choosing a host for your website, I would advise that you use a service that has been around for a while and is proven to be good. As always, read the reviews.

Be sure to have good graphics for your pictures. You want the pictures to be clear and of good resolution, at least 300 dpi. In the beginning you may not be able to afford a photographer, but you can use your phone. Lots of smart phones have good graphics and take very clear pictures. There is also a list of sites that offer free stock photography at the end of this chapter. Also there are lots of programs online—some of them free—that you can use to edit your photos such as Pixlr, Canva, Chalkboard, Color Picker, Craft, Marvel, MockFlow, Design Inspiration, Signature Maker, Placeit and Squarespace Logo, to name a few.

A good website should have a homepage. This is where you would display your logo, business name and slogan. You should include pictures of your products or services and/or service team. Give a description of your business. Let people know your hours of operation. If there are set closing dates such as Christmas Day or July 4th, let people know this too. Give the location of your business and any additional information they may need to find you, especially if your business is difficult to find. And always provide contact information.

Have an "About Us" page. On that page, give a brief description of your business. Customers are interested in knowing your story. They like to know when you started your business, what motivated you, and what you have accomplished so far. So give a little history. You could also include the mission of your business.

The "Contact Us" page is where you would post your physical address, email address, contact numbers and links to your social media sites.

Products and services pages showcase the products and services you provide or offer. If you are selling online, you would need to showcase each individual product, which would be more detailed than if you were not selling online.

Blogs postings can be a great way to drive traffic to your website. It does require some effort and you would need to be committed to posting consistently and regularly. If you are not willing to do so, then a blog may not be a good idea.

WEBSITE BUILDERS

- Bootstrap – One of the most popular front-end frameworks and open source projects in the world, designed to make front-end web development faster and easier.

- Freenom – The world's only free domain provider with a mission to bring people online and help countries develop their digital economy.

- Jimdo – Create a free website with responsive templates, 500MB of storage, unlimited bandwidth. Free plan comes with a Jimdo subdomain.

- Strikingly – Set up a beautiful, free website in under 30 minutes.

- Weebly – Free website builder, e-commerce platform and marketing tools—all in one place.

- Wix – Free website builder with unlimited pages, 500MB storage, secure hosting, drag 'n' drop editor and mobile site.

- WordPress.org – WordPress is free and powers 27 percent of the web. You will need to buy your own domain name and pay for hosting—the latter can be found for as little as $3.95 per month.

- Yola – Free website plan gives you up to 3 pages, 1GB storage and a Yola subdomain.

E-COMMERCE SOLUTIONS

Sell stuff online by joining the most popular online marketplaces or go the DIY route and create your own e-commerce website and collect payments yourself.

- Big Cartel – Build a free online store, sell in-person and run your creative business from one platform.

- Etsy – Sell your handmade or vintage products on Etsy and reach millions of buyers around the world.
- PayPal – A fast, safe way to send and receive money, make online payments and set up a merchant account.
- Square – Sell online via Square's website, your own site or with third party e-commerce sites. All options come with next-day deposits, accepts all major credit cards and integrates your reporting and inventory with your offline sales.
- WooCommerce – Customizable e-commerce platform for building your online business. Integrates seamlessly with WordPress.

TEACH AND SELL ONLINE COURSES

- OpenLearning – An online learning platform with a focus on community, connectedness, and student engagement.
- Skillshare – A global learning community. Take one of thousands of online classes or teach one yourself.
- Teachable – Build a beautiful course website and control your branding, student data, and pricing in one place.
- Thinkific Starter Plan – Everything you need to easily create, market, and sell your own online courses.
- Udemy – Udemy helps with distribution, customer service and payment processing.

STOCK PHOTOGRAPHY

- Death to the Stock Photo – A collection of themed stock photos delivered straight to your inbox.
- Free Nature Stock – Royalty-free nature photos, updated daily.

- Gratisography – Unique high-resolution photos in a range of categories.
- Magdeleine – Get one free, hand-picked, high-resolution photo every day.
- StockSnap – Hundreds of high-resolution images added weekly.
- Streetwill – Free high-resolution vintage photos to use any way you want.
- The Stocks – A collection of the best "non-stocky" stock photo websites, curated in one place.
- Unsplash – Ten new free photos added every ten days, available online or via email subscription.

CHAPTER 12
EMAIL AND SOCIAL MEDIA MARKETING AND ANALYTICS

For I will give you a mouth and wisdom, which all your adversaries will not be able to contradict or resist (Luke 21:15).

Marketing your business does not start after you register your business. Marketing starts from the very beginning when you got your idea and decided to act on it. You should be speaking to others and letting people know about your business so that they could help you spread the word around. If no one knows your business exists, then no one can buy your goods or use your service.

I can recall when I started my first business. I knew nothing about marketing, so on the first day of the launch I expected people to go to my website and purchase my products that I thought were very "nice" and worth buying. But I did not market my products, so no one came to the site that day and many days after that. It took me a long time to figure out that one of the reasons that the business struggled was because I did not market my products. You do not have to make the same mistake.

Traditionally, printed advertising was the way to go, but it is very costly to get your ads in a magazine or mailed to people's homes. Social media has become the new vehicle for advertising. People spend so much time on Facebook, Instagram, Twitter and websites that it only makes sense to target potential clients in these places. Some social media sites are better suited for some businesses than others. We will look at different ways to advertise, and you can choose which way or ways suits you best. Marketing is not a one size fits all.

Email marketing is self-explanatory. It's the use of emails to market products. In order to reach people by email, you would need an email list. You can start with the list of friends and family that you have. You can also build your email list. Here are some tips to growing your email list:

(1) Collect emails by asking people to sign up at events where you are a vendor.

(2) Launch some social media advertising to invite people to sign up. To encourage people to sign up, you may

need to offer them something, such as a coupon/ discount, a free consultation or an ebook. Ask for their emails in exchange for the freebee. Create a landing page that would require them to put in their emails in order for the freebee to be sent to their emails.

(3) You can have an email sign-up on your website that pops up when people visit your website. Also, you can request their email at checkout when they are purchasing from your website.

(4) Add a sign-up button to your Facebook page.

As you are growing your list, the email addresses should be added to the list that you started in an email account such as Constant Contact, Sparkpost or MailChimp. These email marketing programs were designed for small businesses. They are free to use, if you have a small audience under 2000 and your emails per month fall within their limit. I use Mailchimp and it is amazing. I know of other people who use these emailing programs and find them very helpful. I can tell you from experience with Mailchimp that it helps you with automating some of your responses, newsletters, adverts, and a host of other things. Go and browse around on these sites and see which one works best for you.

Your emails need to be compelling. When you are putting together your compelling emails, do the following:

- Have a clear subject line.
- Have a call to action i.e., *"click on the link below to get your free..."*
- Have a great mobile design for mobile devices. Most people use mobile devices and you want to make sure that they have a nice view of your site.

- Have good content. This is where you can source out to someone on sites such as Fiverr. You should have your content personalized to suit your target audience.

- Make sure that the content is proofread for any spelling or grammatical mistakes.

If you want more information on how you can build your email list, you can go on to QuickSprout.com or Udemy.com where you will find teaching programs on how to build an email list.

SOCIAL MEDIA MARKETING

1. **SEO and Website Analytics.** SEO stands for Search Engine Optimization. This means that changes are made to your website design and content to make it appear in your search engines. Optimizing your website makes it more visible in organic or unpaid search results.

2. **SEM Marketing.** This is a type of internet marketing that involves promoting your website by increasing its visibility in search engine results by paid means. You can pay search engines, such as Google and Bing for SEM, and see your website appear on the first pages, instead of on following pages. Most people do not look at second page results. They only look at the first page results when they do their search.

3. **Online Reviews.** When people are faced with a lot of choices as to where to take their business, they first go to sites such as Facebook, Google and Yelp for online reviews. People look to online reviews for honest appraisals.

   Online reviews are similar to word-of-mouth referrals, except that word-of-mouth may be limited to the number of people that will hear the review. Online reviews have the potential to reach a lot of people. Big businesses capitalize on this to build loyal customers. Small businesses, however, do not seem to take advantage of this. Small businesses often stick to more traditional ways of marketing, such as printed ads, leaflets, etc. This is costly, whereas online reviews are free.

For online reviews to work, customers need to be encouraged to write reviews online. You may need to offer something to get people to write a review. Always remember to keep an eye on the reviews online. It's also a good idea to go online and thank the people who write the reviews. Of course this may become difficult to do if the business is being bombarded with lots of reviews. Also, if there is a negative review, you need to deal with it and try to resolve the issue immediately.

4. **Visual Marketing.** Visual marketing is a very powerful tool to use in business, especially at this time when so many people spend so much time on social media. Research has shown that people respond more favorably to pictures, than they do to text only postings or advertisement. The pictures need to be of good quality and visually appealing. Ninety-three percent of the most engaging posts on Facebook are photo posts—*Social Media Examiner.* Visual content is more than forty times more likely to get shared on social media—*Buffer.* Tweets with images received 150 percent more retweets than tweets without images— *Kissmetrics.* Almost 66 percent of updates on social media are visual content—*Quicksprout.*

The stats are clear. Create your marketing content with visually appealing images and you will optimize your presence on social media. Below are some free tools that can help you create beautiful images for your social media sites: Getty Images; Pixlr; What the Font; Paletton; Pik Jumbo; Colorseeds; Free Pik; Colourlovers; Google Web Fonts;

Design-Seeds; Image Color Picker; Ico Moon; Vecteezy; Social Media Image Maker; Vizz Buzz; Skitch; My Poster Wall; Call-to-Action Button Optimizer; Tagexdo; Quoizo; Canva; Clipping Magic; Easel.ly; Infogra.am and Slide.ly

5. **Contests and Giveaways.** Creating a contest on Facebook and Instagram is free and easy. Contests are used to build brand awareness and gain new clients.

   Before starting the contest/campaign, establish a clear goal. Be it increasing posts engagement, promoting a sale or event and/or building you email list, as with all other ads, the contest must have a call to action. It must say what will be awarded to the winner.

6. **Facebook Marketing.** Facebook's organic reach has been reduced from 20 percent to 2 percent. This means that 98 percent of your friends and contacts on Facebook do not see your postings and status updates unless they specifically go searching on your site. In order to boost your reach on Facebook, you would need to go the route of paid advertising. With paid advertising, you have the option to choose the number of people you want to reach, the characteristics, and demographic of those people. Facebook advertising does not cost much, and it also boosts your ratings on places like Google.

   Another effective technique when marketing on Facebook is to use more shareable content. By that I mean use content that people would want to share. For example, hashtag (#) a popular event that people would be interested in such as the Boston Marathon or a past event in which you participated and posted pictures. If I were to use myself as an example, whenever my company, Jewelz on Demand, is a vendor at an event, I post pictures of the event. The likes and shares increase dramatically than when I just post a picture of a piece of jewelry or just text information about the event. Google takes notice of the amount of likes and shares that your posts gets and would reward you by driving more traffic to your page.

This brings us to another point about Facebook. Facebook does not like too much text in advertisements. As a matter of fact, they would not accept an ad with more than 20 percent text. You would need to bear this in mind if you are having someone create a flyer for you.

Facebook Live is a feature that allows people to connect with their contacts live. This feature is being highly used for promotional purposes.

7. **Instagram Marketing.** Instagram is a visually based social media site unlike Facebook and Twitter where a lot of text-based content are shared. Ninety percent of Instagram users are younger than thirty-five years of age (BW), which means this is a good place to go if you are targeting people below the age of thirty-five. It is great for marketing products, building brand awareness and attracting new customers. Unlike other social media sites, Instagram just shows a steady stream of pictures from brands and people you follow. There are no linkages and threads of conversation. Instagram is a good example of visual marketing. The tools listed under visual marketing can be used to create amazing pictures to post on Instagram. Instagram also offers paid advertising.

8. **Hashtag Marketing.** A hashtag is a word or phrase, preceded by the pound or hash sign (#), without any spaces. Hashtags are used on social media to categorize content, making it easier for users to filter and discover content posted elsewhere on social media sites. They are more commonly used on Instagram and Twitter but to a lesser extent on Facebook, Google+ and Pinterest.

When the hashtag sign is added before a word in a social media post, the word or words typed after the # symbol (without spaces) become a clickable link. Users can explore hashtags by either typing a hashtag into a search bar, or simply by tapping or clicking on a hashtag used in a post. When users explore a particular hashtag, they will be shown all posts from public accounts using that hashtag, regardless of whether the user who posted them is following or followed by you.

Use hashtags that are relevant to your business so that you target the people interested in your business or service for example #jewelry. Use popular hashtags but not hashtags that are too popular, though, because they can get buried under hundreds of others. For example, #beadedjewelry would make the search more specific.

Use a limited number of hashtags, such as one to three, on social media sites. Instagram allows up to ten hashtags. On other sites using ten hashtags seems spamy.

Look at hashtags that your audience uses on social media sites. Hashtagers use a lot of abbreviated terms. Find those related to your industry and use them.

Track hashtags that other competitors use. Go on to the competitors' social media sites and see the hashtags that they use.

Go on to **hashtagify.me** to find out the popular hashtags that are being used in your industry. Just type in your industry in the search bar on the site.

9. **Influencer Marketing.** This is a type of marketing that focuses on influential people, rather than the target market. As the name suggests, the influencers are believed to have influence over potential buyers. You would want that person to use or wear your product and post to their social media

site and tag you on the post. This way you can repost on your social media site. If you do not know an influencer personally you may want to get know one by being on their social media site and engaging with them through their posts. Do not ask the influencer to do anything without having engaged with that person for some time. You will know when you can ask them to help you by using your service or product. Consider sending a sample of your product to the influencer for free.

10. **Landing Pages and Lead Capture Pages.** A single landing page or lead capture page is a simple way to build a beautiful sales page, launch countdown or opt-in offer. The following free landing page creators are designed to highlight your best offers and generate more leads. See a list of landing page sites at the end of the chapter.

11. **Google+** is a social networking site owned and operated by Google. It is a free site that has a lot of features. It was intended to compete with Facebook.

12. **LinkedIn** is a business social networking site. It allows you to connect with businesses and professionals that you already know. It is also used by businesses to find and recruit workers and professionals. This site is ideal for coaches, public speakers, counselors and mentors to market themselves. Your profile on Linkedin should be very professional. See it as your personal branding tool. The site is free.

13. **Blog** was coined from the term "web blog." This was an online journal where people would write about the events of their day. Blogging today is used as a marketing tool. Bloggers would talk about events, products, people and current issues generating conversations. There are dedicated blogging websites as well as websites with dedicated blog

pages. Having a blogging page attached to your website is free. Blogging should be done very often if not daily.

Putting together a marketing plan is essential. Devise a plan that works for you and be consistent with implementing the plan. Free marketing plans can be found on coschedule.com. Free marketing training can be found on blog.hubspot.com. It is also important to conduct **Analytics**. In the social media world, this refers to the approach to the collection of data from blogs and social media sites and analyzing them. The analysis data is used to help make business decisions. See free analytics sites below.

ANALYTICS RESOURCES

- Dead Link Checker – Crawls through your site to identify broken links for you to fix.

- Google Alerts – Sets up alerts to track search terms like your name, business, products, etc.

- Google Analytics – Web analytics service that tracks and reports website traffic, giving you valuable insights on your readers and customers.

- Google Keyword Planner – Search and analyze keyword ideas for your Google ad campaigns, or just used to help you brainstorm and optimize your content for search.

- Google Pagespeed Insights – Speed up your website by entering your URL for a free report, plus suggestions for improvement.

- HotJar – All-in-one website analytics and feedback tool that shows you heatmaps, recordings, conversion funnels, and form analysis.

- Keen.io – Developer-friendly APIs that make it easy to collect, explore, and visualize data. Free for usage under $20.00.

- Keywordtool.io – Keyword tool that generates up to 750+ free long tail keyword suggestions.

- Nibbler – Website testing and free report that scores your site based on accessibility, SEO, social media and technology.

- Peek – Free user testing that lets you watch and listen to a five-minute video of a real person using your website.

- Pingdom – Website speed test that measures your site's load time and provides suggestions for improvement.

- SEO Site Checkup – Comprehensive search engine optimization tools for your site, plus a free diagnostic test.

- SimilarWeb – Discover your competitors' website traffic statistics, sources and even their online marketing strategies.

- WordPress SEO by Yoast – Simple WordPress plugin that helps you improve your SEO, write better content and fully optimized your entire WordPress site.

LANDING PAGES AND LEAN CAPTURE PAGES RESOURCES

About.me – A one-page personal website you can set up in just minutes.

Digy – A single responsive HTML5, CSS3 landing page template.

LeadPages Free Templates Resource – The ultimate list of free landing page templates from LeadPages (one of the most popular paid landing page platforms out there). You'll need to code them yourself or hire a developer. Otherwise you can sign up for LeadPages and not touch a line of code.

Releasing the Entrepreneur in You

Landy – A simple and clean responsive landing page template. This one's great for promoting your app, software, physical products or services.

Ontrapages – A landing page creator with flexible templates and an easy-to-use custom page builder to help you boost conversions for any event, product or launch.

Landing Page Analyzer – How effective is your landing page? This free tool will tell you where and how to improve it, so that it performs better.

CHAPTER 13
MANAGING YOUR TIME

I must work the works of Him who sent me while it is day; the night is coming when no one can work. (John 9:4)

This is a big one—time management. There is a myth that the harder and longer you work in your business, the more productive you will be. This is not true. Research has shown that people who work seventy hours a week is no more productive than someone working forty hours a week. Working too many hours will cause you to get more tired and make more mistakes that you later have to correct or resolve.

I believe that good habits need to be developed early on in your business and everyday life. Some of the items below have been mentioned before in an earlier chapter but I want to stress their importance and encourage you to underscore these points:

- **Set some boundaries for yourself.** When you start a business you will go through a period of excitement, but very quickly you may feel overwhelmed with all that needs to be done. And, yes, you are going to find that your day will go beyond the eight hours that you experienced in your regular job. Instead, you are now working twelve-hour days. That is expected to happen, unless you have lots of money or the help of family and friends.

- **Carve out some time to be with family and friends.** While working long hours may be the reality for a while, I would strongly advise that you make spending time with family and friends a priority. Let the long days be the exception and not the rule. You may have to put more time in to deal with a problem or crisis, but do not let this go on for too long.

- **Make time to rest and exercise.** Have some alone-time where you can think and make clear decisions. The brain gets tired when it's overworked, just like the rest of the body, when you are working out. When the brain is tired, you can make lots of costly mistakes. Your productivity decreases. In the 19th century, when factory owners decreased working hours to ten-hour days and then to eight-hour days they noted a marked increase in productivity. When the brain is tired, you end up wasting time on inconsequential things.

There are other health issues that come from a lack of rest and exercise. Studies by Marianna Virtanen of the Finnish Institute of Occupational Health and her colleagues have found that overwork and the stress that result from it, can lead to a lot of other health problems such as impaired sleep, depression, alcoholism, diabetes, impaired memory, and heart disease. Lack of sleep is also known to be a risk factor for weight gain, memory loss, fatigue and the resulting problems that arise from all of the above.

I will confess that when I initially started making jewelry I was doing it for the joy of it, and then turned it into a business. I would find myself up late at night, then would have to go to my regular job the next day. I eventually became chronically tired and sometimes felt unwell because of it. I have since learned to not make jewelry late into the night, and certainly not every night. Since that time, I have not experienced the extreme tiredness that I used to feel.

- ❖ **Try not to make too many big decisions in one day.** I read somewhere that the reason Mark Zuckerberg, Steve Jobs and Barack Obama wore the same color clothes every day is to eliminate one decision that they had to make. The color is already decided because it does not change. Too many decisions make the brain tired. Some experts suggest that there should be no more than three huge decisions in a day. I have no scientific basis for this suggestion, but I just thought to mention it to give you a benchmark.

- ❖ **Delegate when you can and outsource when you have to.** You do not need to spend time on tasks that do not bring in revenue. Have someone else do them if possible and concentrate on tasks that make money.

- **Organize your day in order of importance.** For example, if you have something really urgent you need to get done in the morning, make a rule not to check your emails before noon. If you do, you will get distracted by what other people want and never get to complete what you need to do to keep your business going. Let the phone go to voicemail. If you have someone to answer the call, let them know what they should disturb you for, and when to take a message. You have to control your time. Do not let others control your time.

- **Get spiritual support.** Speak to your pastor about what you believe that God has called you to do, and seek his/her support, especially if it impacts what you are doing in and for the church. You always want to do things decently. If you have a church sister to help pray you through that would be awesome.

- **Make family a priority.** If you have a family, especially with school-aged children, it is important that you take the time to spend with your wife/husband and children. *"Never get so busy making a living that you forget to make a life,"* says the famous Rev Run. If you allow the children to grow up while you are at work, you would have missed some very special and important milestones in their development that you will never get back. So, make the time and cherish these moments. You will be glad you did.

CHAPTER 14
WALKING BY FAITH

And without faith it is impossible to please God (Hebrews 11:6)

It is easy to tell someone to walk by faith when you are not in that space yourself. Walking by faith is like walking with your eyes closed. You know the floor is under your feet, but you cannot see where you are going, or if there are obstacles in your way to cause you to trip. God is like the floor under your feet, but the difference here is that if we keep holding on to his hand, he will lead us across that floor. Will there be obstacles? Sure, there will be, but God knows how to navigate your path in respect to those obstacles. The amazing thing to know is that the trajectory of your path has already been determined for you by God.

No doubt, as humans, we tend to get in the way and try to change that trajectory. The word of God says, "But without faith it is impossible to please Him, for he who comes to God must believe that He is and that He is a rewarder of those who diligently seek him" (Hebrews 11:6). Make no mistake about God's intentions. He will reward you, but you must first believe and trust that he is who he says he is and can do what he says he can do. God is a man of His word. "His word cannot return to him without doing what it said it will do and prosper in the thing for which it was sent (Isaiah 55:11).

As I am writing these words, they are a reminder to me as well. No matter how many times we find ourselves in situations, we are always faced with the challenge of exercising our faith in God.

It was awesome journeying with you through this book. I do hope that you would have received the encouragement as well as the practical tools you need to embark on your entrepreneurial journey. And I sincerely hope and pray that you feel confident that you can do this *thing* to which you have been called.

EPILOGUE

While the aim of this book is not to discuss in depth the politics and the phenomenon of why Christian women are not taking their rightful place in the marketplace, and in some cases, the church and the world, it is, however, worth acknowledging this very damaging trend, even in light of the gains women have made both in the church and in the world. As we look for ways and avenues to further encourage women in the church to rise up and be counted, we should recognize the root causes of the problem, and also let women know that they are not alone in this walk. God is with them every step of the journey.

Women have been held hostage to misguided beliefs and norms for so long that they have come to accept these untruths as truths. They simply do not know any other way. This book is intended to give hope to these women. It is urging them to wake up and take their rightful place in the marketplace, by the power of God. There is already a sense that women are actually waking up to the truth that entrepreneurship is for them too. They have begun to come to grips with the knowledge that God is calling them to greater things. The onus is now on women to face their fears and anxieties, and to push the self-imposed and societal boundaries aside in their quest for true freedom in Christ. Freedom to be heard, affirmed, and celebrated. Freedom to be all that God has uniquely intended them to be.

Women, it is the dawning of a new day, for us collectively, but even more so, for us as minority women in the church, in respect to entrepreneurship. Let us do this *thing* that we have been called to do.

*Resource listings compiled by Marie Forleo

CPSIA information can be obtained
at www.ICGtesting.com
Printed in the USA
FSHW011216200619
59181FS